It's None of My Business,

BUT...

....All things work together for good to them that love God, to them who are the called according to his purpose.

It's None of My Business,

BUT...

Linda Waters

ETHNIC BOOKS * HOUSTON, TEXAS

IT'S NONE OF MY BUSINESS, BUT. . .
An Ethnic Book

ISBN 0-9630887-4-2
Printed in the United States of America

First printing: March 1996

Ethnic Books are published by Ethnic Books. Its trademark, consisting of the words "Ethnic Books" and the portrayal of a black silhouette couple, is registered in the U.S. Patent and Trademark Office and in other countries.

Ethnic Books
P. O. Box 710352
Houston, TX 77271-0352

This book is dedicated to the people whose business is mine:

E. K., Faye, and Chelsea

Other books by Linda Waters
Published by Ethnic Books:

Slices of Chocolate Lives

Little Ebony Readers®
   Muffin Goes to School

~~
1

It's none of my business but... how can a man go through life moving from one woman's house to another, never experiencing the responsibility of his own residence?

I truly believe that every man and woman should experience the joy and consequences of having his or her own place to live, preferably before they get married. There is a large segment of the male population moving from one woman's house to the next woman's house just as part of the process of changing relationships. It's as though living alone has never crossed their minds. Whatever happened to "courting" or dating?

For the single mothers who allow these men to move in, their children suddenly get a new daddy or a new uncle. There seems always to be another woman (or residence) waiting for these men who have never had the responsibility of paying an electric bill or a telephone bill, not to mention rent.

It seems it might be a bit hard for a woman to distinguish between whether her new man likes her or loves her or whether he just needs someplace to stay. The woman should also ask herself, "How long is he going to stay before he packs his one bag (sometimes a piece of luggage and sometimes just a paper bag) and moves on to the next woman's house or apartment, or room, or project dwelling? Is it love or is it home?

Hoboing from one woman's house to another woman's house is not too great for men either, not in the long run. Many men just live with a woman— not committed—give her a little money on payday — some even give a lot of money on payday, but the problem comes in when they don't ever own anything in the house that their money is helping to pay for.

Whenever the man leaves the woman and her house, whether it is walking out on his own or being thrown out, he usually leaves with that one bag, if anything. In other words, moving from one woman's house to the next woman's house, totally uncommitted, is not only a waste of time; it's a waste of money.

Everybody should know the joy, pain, and responsibility of living on his or her own at least once in life — especially before they marry. The biggest hurdle may be the fear of being alone, or fear of failure, but truly there's nothing to fear but fear itself. No matter how much your family loves you or how much someone says it's okay for you to stay with them for a while; the truth is, there is nothing like your own place. God bless the child that has his own.

~~ 2

It's none of my business, but... people should expose themselves (to knowledge, that is).

There is a whole segment of the population who believes that knowledge about various things is going to just fall out of the sky into their minds without their ever studying about it or opening a book or taking a course.

I have a forty-year old friend who never learned how to cook. She took home economics in high school way back in the seventies, but she never opened a cook book. She sat around the classroom and entertained the other students with conversation while they learned to cook and sew. She always said, "I'll learn one day when I get on my own."

Twenty-two years later, my friend still cannot cook and she cannot hem a pair of pants or sew on a button. She never learned on her own to do either of those things. She never took a cooking class or asked a friend or family member to teach her. It seems she is still waiting to just wake up one day and suddenly know how to cook and sew-like knowledge about cooking and sewing or anything else is just going to fall into her head from the sky.

I have always been an advocate for non-credit or personal enrichment courses. There are numerous colleges, universities, trade schools, and other institutions that offer non-credit courses in every area of study that one can imagine. There is no reason for anyone who has ever wanted to learn to do anything not to have learned. Opportunity is all around. There are classes on painting, horticulture, cooking, photography, singing, martial arts, horse-back riding, sewing, computing, writing, and anything you can actually imagine.

Personal enrichment is priceless. The joy that one can feel after accomplishing a special desire is phenomenal. People used to call it going to "night school." I can testify to the fact that there is life in "Night School." New friends and new ideas are there for the asking.

~~
3

It's none of my business, but... the media should stop trying to destroy people just to get a story.

The media report on personal stuff about people that the public really should not have enough free time on their hands to even be interested in. Why do I need to know who went to court to answer charges of giving someone Herpes? Should I really care if and with whom the candidate for the presidency of the United States had a sexual or extra-marital affair?

13

I believe the media's motivation for answering the public's right to know code is just used as an excuse to declare open-season on certain people. People have been systematically destroyed in the media with information about their personal lives that truly should have been kept within the families of these people.

Did I need the media to force Arthur Ashe to announce his HIV status? No, I did not. That information was between Arthur Ashe and his wife and children. There was no reason for the media to force him out of his silence. There was no reason that Ashe's face should have been plastered on the cover of every tabloid and gossip rag in the country. Ashe was the father of a young child and for the media to overly saturate the news outlets with his personal business was morally wrong, an action which should not have been tolerated in this country.

Even radio announcers design and write their monologs to "drop kick" someone in some fashion. They talk on morning radio and say some terrible things about people who do not get the opportunity to respond. News anchor people, who make insulting remarks about people during news stories do not give the subjects of the insults an opportunity to defend themselves.

The American people are going to have to stand up against this kind of media nosiness. People should write letters to the television networks or local stations and let the managers know that they don't appreciate that kind of reporting from anchors. People are going to have to reject the buying of those gossip rags in order for the publishers to get the message to stop publicizing and exploiting the private lives of people.

~~
4

It's none of my business, but... what ever happened to chivalry? Does it still exist for some people and did it ever exist for all?

I opened a door for my ten-year-old daughter at a U.S. Post Office recently, and as usual, I expected her to go in the door from my right side or under my right arm that I held high above her height. Before my daughter could step into the post office, a man ducked his head and ran under my arm and didn't even say, "Thank you" as he entered the post office. I stood there shocked with my mouth open unable to speak. Everything in my Louisiana up-bringing made me want to shout at his back and say, "Come back here and get to the end of this line." How dare he assume I was holding a door open for him while my child stood there, I thought.

The post office incident led me to randomly survey about 20 women on how they felt about men opening doors for them, and ninety-five percent of the women said they had no expectations for a man other than their husbands or mates opening doors for them. One hundred percent of the women surveyed resented a man walking first through a door that they had opened for themselves.

I mean, really, what would make a man walk through a door first that a woman has opened for herself? What makes a man open a door for one woman, but allows the door to close in the face of another woman or person? Is opening a door for another person a gender thing? Are men the only species who are expected to open doors for others?

My Louisiana up-bringing taught me to always respect my elders. As a rule, I always open the door for the elderly and for children regardless of gender or race. I was taught to always speak to the elderly. To this date, I cannot pass an elderly person without saying, "Hi, how are you?"

I used to say it to all elderly people regardless of gender or race, but only African-American people spoke back to me and didn't look at me as though I were crazy.

I mentioned the differences to my sister, and she said, "Speaking to strangers is out of style." No one else walks around shaking hands and greeting strangers except "country" people or people who are in the same organizations or communities.

Nevertheless, I am so used to opening doors for myself that when a stranger does open a door for me, I say, "Thank you" because I know they could have easily turned the door loose.

I ask, "Do thin women get assistance from men quicker than not-so-thin women? Do white women get doors opened or flat tires changed by all men quicker than African-American women or Asian women or Hispanic women?

I was traveling in my car following my daughter's school bus from a field trip we had taken, when, suddenly, a tire on my car blew out.

Controlling the wheel and pulling onto the shoulder of the road, I didn't have time to signal to the bus ahead of me that I needed help. I panicked because the school bus was going to arrive at my daughter's school, and I would not be there to pick her up.

I parked my car securely and opened the trunk in search of a spare tire. To my dismay, I discovered I had forgotten how to use the portable jack that came with my Honda. I surveyed the area and saw a near-by chemical plant of sorts that sat a few hundred yards away from the freeway. I saw a security guard driving a security vehicle from the feeder into the gate of the plant. I yelled to him from the freeway, then, I began to run towards him until he responded.

I told him I had a flat tire and I had forgotten how to use the jack. I asked him if he could show me how to use the jack and that I would fix the flat myself.

He looked at me without an ounce of sympathy and said that he could call someone for me, but he couldn't help me.

There I was almost thirty miles out of town, my husband was at work at least an hour from me, and the school bus was moving like a steam roller heading for the school without me.

I was disappointed in him as a man and as a human being. I said, "No, thank you. There is no one to call." I wondered whether he had said 'no' because he and I were of different races. I had to dispel that thought because I had no proof.

19

He drove off and I walked back to my car. By this time, I'm mad as hell. I was mad enough to pick up the Honda and hold it on my knee with one hand and change the tire with the other hand.

I took everything out of the trunk of my car, piled it on the side of the road, and I pulled the spare tire from the trunk.

By this time, a man driving an eighteen-wheeler passed me and looked back through the cab to acknowledge me while blowing his horn. For a moment, I thought he was someone I knew. This man pulled onto the shoulder of the road about a half mile away from me. He slowly backed up on the feeder in spurts. It took him several minutes to reach me. I stood there smiling, feeling the hurt and anger towards the security guard seep away.

I was so happy to see help coming. He stepped down from the truck and immediately took charge. I explained about the school bus and about the security guard who wouldn't help me. Not only did the trucker show me how to use the jack, he changed the flat tire.

He said that there was no acceptable excuse for the security guard not helping me. He said he had seen women stranded with car problems on the road all across the United States, some alone, some with children, but he couldn't figure out what makes some men stop to help some women and not stop to help others. "Every time I see a woman stranded, I try to stop and help her because the road is a dangerous place to be," he said. "But I really make an extra effort to help a woman stranded with little children. I have sisters out there; it's the least I can do. Somehow, I feel like if I help somebody's sister, someone may help mine one day."

I offered to pay him for changing the tire, but he said, "Kindness should have no money requirements and I don't charge you a dime. Just get to the school to see about your child."

I shook his hand and, then, he was gone. I can honestly testify that sometimes...once in a while...chivalry is not dead!

~~
5

*It's none of my business, but...
It is a shame that the very people
who benefited from Affirmative
Action are not supporting it now
and in most cases are voting
against it.*

There would never have been a need for
Affirmative Action if we lived in a prejudice-free
and equal opportunity country. Everyone on the
planet knows that America has inflicted numerous

injustices against all minorities at one period of time or another. Every race labeled under the heading "minority" was enslaved, exploited, imprisoned immorally, or just "kept back" economically in this country.

First of all, the program should never have been called Affirmative Action, because it was designed to correct an economic imbalance in our society. Therefore, the program should have been called "The Equalizer."

For President Nixon to have signed Affirmative Action into law speaks to the very need of such a program then and now. There are industries and companies that serve all people in this country; yet, many of these companies only hire white people. Many Affirmative Action opposers don't seem to find anything wrong with that. Some water companies that collect money from every family in a sub-division, regardless of color, choose only to hire white people. This is racial discrimination and it should be against the law. However, you have a large segment of the population who feels there is nothing wrong with that.

The *Angry White Male Syndrome* took off and gained fuel throughout America mainly because people who have never had to deal with their neigborhoods being "red-lined" or denied an employment application to work in a company whose "bosses" openly joke about not intergrating the work-place are very much in power. People from the grocery store to city hall to the House of Representatives to Congress to the White House and all the way to the Supreme Court are fighting Affirmative Action when it was created to be an opportunity to a group of people who would always be systematically shut out regardless of qualifications. People born into a group having 99% of the pie started the cry against Affirmative Action. They're bitching about wanting the last one percent that is divided among all United States minorities (and not equally among them). I say U.S. minorities because each race such as Asians, Africans, Hispanics, and others that fall under the heading of minority in the United States is a majority in his or her native country.

People are complaining because it was necessary for the federal government to force companies to open doors that had been permanently closed to minorities.

Minorities of many races were systematically shut out of jobs in companies that government dollars fuel and keep alive. There are companies that make a large part of their revenue from minority consumers; yet they refused to hire any minorities until Affirmative Action.

It is even sadder when minorities and women of all races who have benefited from Affirmative Action now stand with their "job security" and speak out against, vote against, and just plain put down the very tool they used to the maximum just to get a chance, not ahead. Judge Clarence Thomas who benefited educationally from Affirmative Action was quoted in the *Houston Chronicle* as saying, "It's time to put that genie back into the bottle."

I wonder how people who got in the door and over the door can sleep at night after cementing the door shut to those coming behind them? I really feel badly when I think about the true civil rights fighters who were poor and uneducated, who gave their pennies, their time, their homes, their food, their blood, their hope, faith, and prayers for the movement so that their children could have opportunities that were denied them because of race. I feel angry because what they fought for did not benefit their children, but somehow benefited the children who now think the country doesn't need Affirmative Action. Those children reaped the fruits of labor that their parents did not sow, and as soon as they got their Affirmative Action degrees and their Affirmative Action jobs, they ceased to have anything positive to say about it. All of a sudden, they want to adopt the philosophy of the "Angry White Male Syndrome and say things like, "Our people don't want charity, no hand-outs; we want to be treated equally and really earn what we get. Enough with Affirmative Action; it's just not right. We don't want to make allowances for minorities any more."

If each race of people were counted individually like Africans or blacks, Hispanics or Mexicans, every race would have a shot at the title "majority." The white race is comprised of Italians, Greeks, Germans, Poles, Irish, and all who look "European." However, the true number count of each race of people without combining races for a larger number count would soon put an end to that old American saying, "Majority Rule."

It's enough to make you sick to know America invented and practices a double-standard in almost every avenue of life. Even the two-faced professionals who directly benefitted from Affirmative Action also subscribe to the practice of a "double-standard" when they think they are free from being poor and shut-out. To all of those people, I say with all honesty, "Until all people are free, no one anywhere is free. You, too, may be just a job away from living in the project or under the freeway. Be careful my brother, my sister; you haven't gotten ovah yet."

~~
6

It's none of my business, but...
I truly believe a beauty salon is
a place for hair customers and
hair customers only.

Too many times I have walked into hair salons where non-customers are just sitting all over the shop. These people are either family or friends of the actual customers or workers in the hair salon. They lie down in the salon, eat huge containers of exotic-smelling foods and feel free to walk around with these open containers of food in a place that is filled with pieces of cut hair.

I recently had my hair done in a salon by my favorite stylist. I go to her because she does to my hair exactly as I request and I was a hairdresser long enough to know that this is rare. But in this day and age, where businesses are competing for the dollar without a conscience, it is totally destructive to business to allow customers, family, or friends to bring into the salon three and four children who are not getting their hair done. It is outrageous to think that paying customers can enjoy or endure that kind of chaos for a long period of time.

By the time my hair was rolled for the permanent wave, I had to leave the salon for a break. I had witnessed enough chaos with twelve children running around the salon, dropping food all over the place and crying and fussing among themselves. Baby strollers, walkers, and playpens were all over the salon. Trash cans running over with trash and garbage, chemical odors, and loud talking dominating the scenery was too much for me under the best conditions. Spending several hours in a hair salon getting a hair service can be too much for most people. I want peace and calm in a salon. I went to a nearby restaurant and used the drive-thru to get lunch. I ate the food in my car instead of in the salon, and I sat in my car until I felt the processing time on my permanent wave had passed before I returned to the salon.

I can only say that one absolutely has to love the work of a hair stylist in order to frequent a salon which is that chaotic. A hair salon is supposed to be a place of peace and relaxation, because after the hair service is completed, a client is expected to dole out substantial amounts of money for beauty services. Peace and a soothing atmosphere have to be considered for the priceless gift that they bring to the client.

Beauty salons used to be places where pampering took place. A lady could lie back in the chair, listen to soft music, and overhear a little gossip while someone shampooed her hair. In many instances, a client could feel relaxed enough to fall asleep. All I can asked is, "What happened?"

~~7

*It's none of my business, but...
living in an imperfect world of
not-so-perfect people, you can
easily get accustomed to bad
service, products that don't last,
broken appointments, and make-
do, make-shift attitudes from
everyone you encounter.*

Suddenly, when you meet someone who is
perfect at going out of his way to do the right thing
and being all he can be, it can either make you

groan or make you cheer, depending upon the kind of person you are. I cheered when I ran into an old friend recently. I will call him Clyde. Clyde is and has always been a perfectionist.

Even as a child, Clyde established his style. His mother tells stories of his wearing starched dress shirts and bow ties from the time he was nine-years-old to adulthood. In college, he traded the bow ties in for long neck ties. Early on, he chose the clean-cut look because he liked the politeness and respect it generated from people. Shoes shined, mustache trimmed, nails manicured, and every hair in place were his criteria and discipline for himself.

No matter what others do, he always performs to his own impeccable standards. There are many times he stays awake all night completing his work projects only to arrive at work the next day the only one with completed work. He never complains when his colleagues are given extra days to do the same work. Still, the very next time he is expected to turn in work on a specific date, he always delivers.

Clyde received a lot of resentment from his siblings while growing up. As the eldest child, he established a scholastic pace that was almost impossible for his siblings to compete with. Instead of slowing down in his adult life, he shifted gears and accelerated his performance as an employee.

He recognized and felt the envy and snickers from his colleagues, but he chose to endure the territorial punishment to reap the accomplished satisfaction of a perfectionist. Regardless of the loneliness and isolation that soaring above the pack brings, he is a constant in his quest for an unblemished life.

I don't mean to imply that there are not disadvantages in being a perfectionist, working with a perfectionist, or caring for a perfectionist. I've learned to recognize Clyde for all that he is. As a friend, I've managed to benefit from all that makes him a perfectionist and, yet, maintain who I am. I recognize when he needs kind reassurance, usually after someone has misunderstood him and taken personal offense to his being a perfectionist. I just step forward and pat him on the shoulder, reminding him that his greatest reward has to come from within, and that it's okay to walk alone.

~~8~~

It's none of my business, but... home training isn't being taught at home any more.

From countless rude encounters, I have been forced to say that lessons in manners or "home training," as it was called when I was a child should definitely be taught again.

In this day and age, it was hard for me to believe that adults didn't have "home training" until I witnessed numerous incidents that left me shocked. I had no idea that grown men and women would come into your home and simply pick up your mail or your work and begin to read it in your face. I never thought one had to hide one's own mail or purse when people stopped by your home.

When I was a child, and we were in route to someone's house with my mother, she would take a moment before our departure and say, "I want y'all to behave when we get where we're going. I don't want y'all to grow up and become the kind of people that folks pretend they're not home when they look up and see you coming."

My mother's favorite line to us was, "There is a big difference in being in your own house as opposed to being in someone else's house. Things you do at home, you just can't do away from home. You should never go into anyone's refrigerator, even with permission. You can't ever eat or drink the last of anything unless it is offered by the owner. Only your mama and daddy will give their last "cracker" or drink. I want y'all to know that because you have to go away from home one day."

I remember my mother having a certain look that she gave us that told us immediately what her answer was to what ever we were puzzled about. If people offered us something to eat in their homes, we would first look at my mother before we would answer. Most times, showing good manners, we would simply say, "No thank you." My mother said these things over thirty years ago, and over the years, I simply thought everyone's mother said those things until recently. I could not imagine grown folks going into someone's refrigerator without being invited, yet, I've encountered too many folk who take liberties in other people's homes and businesses. I really cringe every time I see people come in from outdoors and go straight to someone's refrigerator without washing their hands. The first thing they do after grabbing a glass is to put their unwashed hands in the ice bin to get ice for a drink, leaving dirt and possible germs on the ice. I just want to scream out, "Excuse Me, but how can you not know better than that. Your mama didn't give you any home training?"

I teach my children not to touch anything on anyone's desk when we have the occasion to visit a business office, but the fact is, every desk, whether in someone's home or a bank, should be treated with respect such that nothing is touched by others without an invitation or permission.

It is expected that one would teach a child not to eat or drink behind anyone and to wash his hands after a bathroom visit. The shock to me is when you have to make that statement to an adult.

I have lost track of how many times I've witnessed adults using public restrooms and leaving without washing their hands. People are much too generous with their germs. Young children are learning manners from observing adult behavior. "Home training?" That was what manners were called years ago because most people learned them while still living at their parents's home. I believe we should return to that custom.

~9~

It's none of my business, but... after shopping recently in a local drugstore, I believe parents need to bring back the "paddle" and the "switch," or at least the threat of them.

Parents need to discipline their children, especially in public. If someone allows his child to tear up his home, that's his business, but children should not be allowed to tear up stores and other people's property. Society cannot and should not bear the brunt of the antics of undisciplined children. Now, I know a lot of you (mostly non-parents) are going to get angry at that statement, but please hear me out.

I was a prescription-buying, money-spending customer in the drugstore just like the parents of some hollering, kicking, screaming, shelf-destroying, product-tampering children, but I, like all other shoppers in that store, was a victim of this uncontrolled circus.

The pharmacist on duty explained to prescription shoppers that there would be a twenty-minute wait. My head suddenly began pounding when I realized that I had to spend twenty additional minutes in that chaotic environment. Now, had I been shopping for a prescription for myself, I would have left the prescription at the store and returned the next day for pickup, but the prescription was for my baby and I wanted her to start on her prescription that day. At that point, I took my older daughter and struggled through the line of people, careful not to step on customers' wandering, and yes, crawling babies about the floor.

While my daughter and I sat together in one of three chairs in the waiting area, we watched unattended children pull products from shelves, destroy store displays, open packages, and play with the contents while children who appeared ill screamed, sneezed, coughed, and cried at the prescription counter. All of this went on while their parents stood idly at the counter as though their children's behavior was acceptable.

I watched the sales clerks pick packages off the floor and constantly clean and restock the areas that kids had destroyed. The parents of these kids never tried to clean up or restock anything that their kids had destroyed. None of the children was sent back to the displays to restock the products or clean up the mess they had made.

When I got home, I phoned the store manager and told her of my headache from the chaos and the uncontrolled children in the store. I was too upset to wait until she could see me in the store. She apologized for my headache and experience in the store and thanked me for my comment, but she told me that there was absolutely nothing that she or the store clerks could do. She said that when she and store clerks have approached parents about the noise and destructive behavior of their kids in the store, they have been cursed, screamed at, and insulted by the parents and, then, reported to the regional office of the drugstore. She explained to me that the regional office management has prevented them from saying anything to disruptive parents and children in the store. I asked for the address of the regional office, because I feel that they are protecting the rights of the wrong people. Paying customers who are not disruptive need the store to realize how they feel when there is no order in a store. I feel it is wrong for store clerks to have to clean behind other people's children. I believe parents are setting terrible examples for their children when they allow them to destroy merchandise in a store and, then, argue with the management when told about it.

I have witnessed some clerks in fabric stores asking kids to leave items alone. I applaud the management of such stores. Sometimes people go shopping to be at peace, not to have other people's children running all over them. I believe children should be forced to behave in public. Everyone should not be aggravated in a business by other people's kids who are disruptive and destructive.

It's none of my business, but...I don't believe I am alone in feeling this way.

$\tilde{1}\tilde{0}$

It's none of my business, but... what ever happened to "You are innocent until proven guilty" in the United States of America?

I ask that question not just because O.J. Simpson was charged with two counts of murder, but for every person that has been accused of anything. Take for instance, the arrest of a public figure in Houston whom I shall call Charles. Charles was arrested for DWI, and every local station in Houston sensationalized it on the morning, noon, and evening news. Like O.J., before Charles had his day in court, he was already tried and found guilty in the eyes of many. Yet, it was not up to Charles to prove his innocence. That should have been a given. It was up to the district attorney's office to prove Charles's guilt from whatever evidence they had.

Suddenly, the very next day, the district attorney in Houston dropped all charges against Charles because the evidence that the police obtained was not sufficient to convict Charles for DWI. Many people questioned by the media were recorded as having said, "Now, we will never know if Charles were innocent." I say, "Something is wrong when a statement is phrased that way. Charles, as well as everyone else, should be considered innocent until proven guilty."

It seems that an impressive reputation and a winning career that took a lifetime to build can be torn down in less than fifteen minutes in the media. Why is the public so eager to believe the worst about a person? Why is the public so eager to believe the media and even the police without waiting until all the evidence is in and the final summations are made? The policemen don't spend time trying to prove the accused innocent; that's not their job. The public doesn't, nor do the media spend time trying to prove the innocence of an accused; so who does? If an accused person doesn't have enough money to hire investigators and lawyers to prove his innocence, he can very well go to jail and sit there until the trial without ever having commited a crime.

Looking at what has happened to O.J. Simpson and Charles, two men with public personas, finances, friends, and lawyers, I hate to think about the irrevocable damage that can be done to innocent, poor people who are accused of crimes in this society. It seems that the media immediately swallow them up and good citizens stand by and "amen" all the information from day one without looking beyond the hype. That is the real crime to me, because even after charges are dropped against a "suspect," (someone who is accused of a crime, but not convicted) the media and the gossiping public never give "dropped charges" as much lip service as they did the accusation. It makes me say, "Ooh, but to be poor and accused in this country." Just the thought of it brings to mind what Mr. T. (Lawrence Theo, formerly of The A Team) is known for saying, "I pity the fool."

It's none of my business but. . .people should think about how they would feel accused of a crime and suddenly convicted by the whole world without due process of the law and without ever having gone to trial to defend themselves.

~~
11

It is none of my business, but... the silence of the babies in Rwanda is deafening to the heart.

My seeing the sick, dying babies from Rwanda on television makes me cry. I grew up in a place surrounded by adults who risked life and limb to save a child, anybody's child. I live in a country where man walks the moon, atoms are smashed, and the world of communications has allowed us to say, "There is no there—only here." All of my past has made me who I am, and who I am makes me want to save the children—my children, Rwanda's children, Bosnia's children, anybody's children, everybody's children.

The sadness of watching suddenly orphaned, sick children wandering through the camps without a tear or the sound of a sob is heart-breaking. Nothing I've learned prepares me for acceptance or comprehension of a child who doesn't cry. It's hard to imagine a child having had such horrendous experiences until he presumes that crying brings no one to solve the problem. All a baby can do to communicate pain or to solicit help is to cry. A cry from a baby is a symbol of trust that demonstrates that the baby expects someone to come. When babies stop crying or never start to cry, it makes me feel that the whole world has let them down.

The children of Rwanda don't seem to cry because they may believe that no one is coming. I've seen the news footage from Rwanda where the children just lie down and die without a tear or a sob. It makes me ask myself, "What kind of world is this if we can't save the children." Men walking on the moon, the Concord flying from New York to London in less than four hours, an over abundance of diamonds and gold in the world, black crude oil shooting out of the ground, and the introduction and promotion of the Super Highway mean very little to poor, sick, dying children. The children not only seem unimpressed, they are unaware. Materialism should never win over life.

Children are our future. They are being shaped and groomed by the world's greed and misplaced priorities. The tears of the children are drying up world-wide as they watch us do nothing. The tears are connected to the heart, and the heart is connected to the soul and spirit. The souls and spirits of these tearless, dying children are at risk and are bound to have an effect on us as we watch.

The television pictures are in our homes, and I wonder why families world-wide can't reach out and help, even adopt an orphaned child. "Red tape" should not play a part in matters of the heart. Those children need immediate attention, both medically and emotionally. We need adults to save the children, any body's children, everybody's children.

It's none of my business, but I cry for the sick, dying children, because I still hope and believe someone will come at the sight of a tear and the sound of a sob. I hope you do, too.

~~
12

*It's none of my business, but...
the contract with America seems
to target government welfare
reform, but only selectively.*

I believe that if Republicans really wanted to
reform welfare, they would start with politicians
instead of with kids. I don't have any objections to
my tax dollars being used to feed hungry kids when
their parents are not able to do their jobs. What I
have a problem with is having my tax dollars spent
on supporting ex-presidents and their families

and ex-politicians' retirement funds and office perks.

I consider government subsidy as a "big federal checking account," and as I see it, money to support ex-presidents along with secret-service protection, and ex-politicians' perks come out of that same big federal checking account that welfare for women and children come from. The difference is, I expect the ex-presidents to have enough money to take care of themselves and not have to accept money from the government. Certainly, one would expect the former president of the United States of America to have more money than a woman and child on welfare.

Why is it okay for the government to support former presidents, supply retirement funds for former senators and representatives, but not pay for school breakfast for poor kids whose families fall below the poverty line? Medical care, office rent, office staff, and secret service protection for former presidents (at one time we had five living) certainly total far more than the cost of feeding breakfast to hungry school children.

It seems that former senators and other politicians who were voted out of office this past election still held onto their government funded guaranteed-retirement funds even after leaving

Washington, D.C. CBS news reported ousted politician Dan Rostenkowski leaving Washington, D.C. with an intact pension plan of more than $123,000 even though the voters voted him out of office. How many kids and welfare mothers are going to get that kind of pension plan when the government cuts them off from the "big government checking account" in the sky? Do you think that is fair?

I truly can understand the Republicans preaching the idea that every tub should sit on its own bottom, but shouldn't that apply to every tub and every bottom? When are the politicians proposing the welfare reform going to sit on their own bottoms? They are living off the "big government checking account" in the sky.

It's none of my business, but...I am almost certain that I am not the only taxpayer who feels that way. How about you?

~~
13

It's none of my business, but... I really wish the Arsenio Hall Show and the Whoopi Goldberg Show would come back to television.

I won't say that the Arsenio Hall Show or the Whoopi Goldberg Show should not have been canceled, because both shows probably had to leave the airwaves for some people to realize just how important the shows were to the American culture. The shows added diversity, fairness, and respect to guests who otherwise would never have been seen on television. Legendary celebrities who are no longer making movies and no longer recording music were welcomed with a respect and fondness by Arsenio Hall and Whoopi Goldberg that few entertainers ever know. All races of people were welcomed to these shows as guests. Many people were able to see and hear their childhood idols and know and learn what they had been doing over the years.

The Late Show with David Letterman and the Tonight Show with Jay Leno are formatted with a unique style that only seems to have a spot for actors and music makers who have current products to promote. Then, sadly, these chosen guests are only allowed a short period of time to tell some kind of joke, hype their products and leave. The guest spot is so quick it seems almost a waste of the celebrities' time to leave their homes to do the show. The celebrity may as well hook up to a satellite feed from his home for those ten minutes at the most. Click, click, and it's over.

Maybe, I'm yearning for a talk show where people actually sit and exchange meaningful intellectual chatter so much until I cannot appreciate two or three carefully rehearsed sound bytes that are supposed to come across as spontaneous repartee, but doesn't.

Real people talking about real concerns is

what is missing in late night television, and Arsenio Hall and Whoopi Goldberg brought that to America, and they brought it with style.

I can never forget seeing Eartha Kitt on the Whoopi Goldberg Show. Eartha was so vivacious and informative about the years in which she was black-balled from America as an entertainer. She spoke without bitterness and she described her White House visit with the Johnsons that turned into an ugly public scene in America. Eartha never stopped proclaiming her love for America as she recalled her troubles.

Whoppi Goldberg's show was actually a place where a guest could talk and do it (most of all) without a studio audience and without being interrupted and totally interpreted by Whoopi, which so many other talk-show hosts so rudely do. Billy Crystal shared his experiences in portraying Sammy Davis, Jr. with a crooked smile and told the audience about the time he found out that Sammy was offended by the portrayal. Whoopi allowed him to tell his story without her summing it up for the audience. Billy Crystal said that he admired and loved Sammy Davis, Jr. and only wanted to portray him out of admiration.

The Arsenio Hall Show, on the other hand, was as wonderful with a studio audience as Whoopi's Show was without one. I loved seeing Robin Williams having time to talk and tell many jokes

love the children they are hauling, but I am saying that they are certainly risking the lives of these children.

It makes me very nervous and extremely perplexed when I see pretty little boys' and girls' faces sticking out of the car windows such that I can almost count the eyelashes on their eye lids. Many times I've considered rolling my car window down and shouting at the kids to put their bodies back into the cars. Apparently, many adults have not heeded the warning of the consequences of not buckling up in seat belts. Maybe, society should spend some advertising dollars toward creating commercials that give that information to the children out there who are riding in cars without buckling up in seatbelts. Maybe with the proper instructions, children of a certain age can begin to take care of themselves by always buckling themselves in seat belts whether an adult reminds them or not.

Lately, during business hours, I've been seeing a lot of men riding around drinking beer, music blasting, car windows rolled down, and children hanging dangerously out of the windows. I often wonder if they are paid by some family member to babysit or are they the fathers of these children? It is very painful to drive in the face of that kind of shameful horror and not be able to say anything to the people who are doing wrong by children. I truly wonder if they love the children or wish to do well by them, but just don't know any better about the wrong they're doing.

When I was a child, I lived in a part of the world and during a time when an adult could walk up to another adult, sometimes younger, and offer advice on child care, child rearing, or just general information on safety and remedies. At that time, most parents were happy to get the information and usually said, "Thank you." Now, we live in a time that if you honk your car horn behind some people at the traffic light, you're subject to be shot before you can drive on. In applying that to this instance, one has to wait for the police to get involved and ticket these drivers who endanger the lives of children in moving vehicles rather than take matters into one's own hands.

Waiting until someone has an accident and injures or kills a child is the wrong time to try to teach that person a lesson on the law. Jailing an adult who injures a child in an automobile accident or mishap does not undo the physical damage and sometimes death that happens to children when an accident occurs. Bodies flying out of the car can be fatal, and kids sitting in the laps of other passengers are used as body shields in a collision impact.

In all honesty, the safest place for a child in a car is strapped in a car seat or buckled in a seat belt until the driver has reached his or her destination. It's as simple as all that. I simply wish the police would intervene and place the kind of astronomical fines on drivers that would make them never drive carelessly with children hanging out of vehicle windows again.

~~15

It's none of my business, but... role modeling should begin at home.

I am tired of hearing people talk about role models for "poor children?"

You don't hear people suggesting role models for rich folk's children, or even many middle-class (whatever that is these days) folks' children. It seems that only these "poor children without a father," and these "poor children from the bad neighborhoods" are the ones most folks want to give a role model to. I ask, "What role models do 'poor little rich children' have? Who do they look up to in order to stay away from drugs or stay out of psychiatrists' offices? Whom do they look up to to reach the world's definition of success?"

The tiredness comes to me when people go on to say, "poor Black children" should look up to successful Blacks and poor little Hispanic children should look up to successful Hispanics, and then these same people go on to define "successful" as an athlete, actor, comedian, recording star, or rapper who was "lucky" enough or "blessed" enough to earn millions of dollars for something they enjoy doing. What does money have to do with role-modeling? You don't have to be rich to teach a child how to care about himself and other people.

The trouble with suggesting and promoting famous wealthy people as role models for "poor children" is that people create two extremes for the children without any middle ground or steps. The distance from poverty to wealth is long. Who is going to fill that huge gap in the middle? Children need bridges to get from one level to the next. That's where "everyday people" come in.

Children should not spend their precious school years looking for that "lucky break" with their eyes focused only on the famous wealthy minorities and their lifestyles for the few minutes a week that the famous folks are on television. The questions are: "What does the child do with the rest of his time that day, week, month, or year? Who helps a child to lay the proper foundation to build a future?"

Parents, family, neighbors, friends, and people who are going to be a physical part of a child's life must unite and begin to build a structure with a solid realistic foundation in order for that child to grow into a positive, productive adult.

Telling a child that he can grow up and be "like Michael Jordan," or any other professional athlete, actor, or famous person without helping him to construct steps or the path it takes to get there is both dangerous and cruel. Society (people) should not dominate a child's mind with images of rich and famous people listed under the column entitled, "successful," if they are not going to actually help that child build a future.

Think about all the recording artists who sang themselves into bankruptcy, drugs, and some even back into the neighborhoods from which they fled. Some admit today that they did not have the "smarts" to handle their own affairs. Where were their education and skills that could have sustained them in life? How can children obtain that "big money" if they don't make it as a "star?" Chasing stardom without the proper hands-on guidance can leave children with the options that can lead them to jail, drugs, or death. Pushing "poor children" to the notion of super-stardom without teaching them immediate, obtainable goals that will sustain them and support them is setting "poor children" up for a fall.

Parents must put themselves in the glowing spotlight of their children's eyes. Parents should be the first and most important role models for their own children. Rules, manners, and morals should be taught at home while the children are young enough to have time to try out the lessons and, hopefully, master them before they are turned out into the world at eighteen or sometimes younger. A child has to be able to look at his parent or parents with respect and not look at them and compare them and what they have to the "big money" and lifestyles of "rich people." It should matter to the child how these so-called "successful" people made their money. Then, children would stop glamorizing drug dealers, pimps, prostitutes, rogues, and one-dimensional images of people who they see on television. The real world demands that children understand early on that they must get a jump on getting a firm foundation.

It doesn't matter what a famous person says to other people's children about "staying off drugs" and "staying in school" if those rules and morals are not taught at home. If a parent doesn't agree and doesn't practice the instructions, whom do you think they child is going to respond to? Children are getting conflicting messages from parents, society, peers, and so-called famous people. Children should acknowledge the people who are living the simple, obtainable lifestyles and view those "superstars" just as they should be viewed — simply sources of entertainment.

The chance of a "superstar" actually helping a child would be greater if children were allowed to share a closer, personal relationship with famous people who wish to be around the children and help to create a realistic purpose in those children's lives. Guidance, reality and the humanistic elements of life could be exchanged between child and superstar. That untouchable fantasy would become real and the "superstar" could talk to the kid as a person and dispel any myths the child might have about the reality of "obtainable superstardom" in America. Also, "superstars" have children of their own who have publicly acknowledged that fame has its price. Children should know that. Life can be fulfilling without great wealth. It has to be. Less than 1% of 32 million Black (far less than 320,000) people in America are considered "wealthy." That means that the other 31,000,000 people have to learn to live below, at, or slightly above the poverty line.

Little girls growing up dreaming about becoming beauty queens and career women without doing the work — getting an education and striving for obtainable goals first along the journey-can lead to a dangerous level of inadequacy when those fairy tales don't materialize. Inadequacy creates vulnerability and gullibility that weakens one's control and self-esteem. Realistic goals achieved help strengthen self-esteem and build hope. That combination bridges the gap.

So, I say, come on parents, lawyers, ministers, teachers, nurses, doctors, social workers, writers, journalists, engineers, builders, bankers, secretaries, cooks, seamstresses, entrepreneurs, and next-door neighbors who work to help build this country, you must take a stand. I ask that you get busy and introduce your professional industries to young children so that they can know there are other sustaining and enriching occupations in the world besides entertainment.

~~
16

It's none of my business, but... something has to be done about these women who actually apply make-up to their faces while they drive a car.

     I refer to this person as a her, because women are usually the people I have witnessed applying makeup and combing their hair while operating a motor vehicle. Whether it has to do with time or just plain boredom while driving, it is positively dangerous to all involved to put on mascara and lipstick, not to mention a full-head brushing at the traffic light.

It's bad enough that people are guilty of talking on cellular phones while driving cars. That, too, is dangerous, but seems a little more acceptable than looking in the mirror with a mascara wane up to their eyes instead of watching the road. A driver does not have to look at his phone in order to talk into it, however, his or her concentration can be affected by engaging in a phone call while driving.

People who are driving and watching other drivers apply make-up or talk on the phone can lose control of their vehicles and collide with other cars, too. People should keep their eyes on the road and not in other people's cars. But it is hard not to notice someone getting dressed and made-up in a car next to or in front of you on a public street.

If you wake up too late to apply your make-up at home, you should wait until you get to the office to apply it or go without it. In essence, no one should risk his life or risk messing up his face so that no make-up can ever fix it. A moving car is no place to apply make-up, and a few seconds at a traffic light is not enough time to apply make-up either.

Unless it is life or death or some type of emergency situation, people should not drive (some at high rates of speed) and talk on the phone at the same time. If you're that important that people have to be in touch with you at all times, you should have a driver or, at least, own your own time enough to be able to stop your vehicle and make a call without endangering your important self or anyone else.

As for applying make-up while driving, women should have come farther than that in this day and age. Women should be beyond risking their lives, their children's lives, and the lives of others for the purpose of arriving at their destinations with make-up intact. It's not worth it no matter who you are or who you think you are. You're playing with a loaded gun. Let's be smarter than that.

~~17~~

It's none of my business, but... it's who you know that makes a difference.

There is an old expression that says, "all successful people over fifty-years old know each other," or there is the expression, "as soon as a person becomes successful, other successful people suddenly want to get to know him?

Regardless of which one of those statements you believe is true, I believe, becoming successful should be important to you, and getting to know other people who are successful or who are aspiring to succeed should be high on your agenda.

If you wait until that boy or girl who sat next to you in high school or sat next to you in two or three college classes makes it to Capitol Hill or Capitol Records, you'll have a difficult time trying to introduce yourself to him then. It's easier to begin networking in your youth. Surround yourself with people who live productive and positive lives.

High school, college, family connections and churches are the best places to start those introductions and begin building those everlasting relationships with other upwardly-mobile, positive-thinking people. At your fingertips is a major network of potentially productive colleagues and future business partners and clients. All one has to do is reach out and introduce oneself to future judges, doctors, scientists, writers, and teachers.

Universities make strong efforts to bring to the campuses a wide range of speakers who are willing to hand out literature about ways people can help themselves. Students should take advantage of whatever guests and talent that the universities bring to them. Learn to network with people who are productive before finishing college. You may be surprised one day to suddenly realize who you know.

~~
18

It's none of my business, but... I believe that every woman should exercise her right to vote.

I grew up knowing that people died so that African-Americans and, later, women could vote, and I couldn't wait until I turned eighteen to exercise that right. I didn't want those who fought to have died in vain.

We're living in the age when laws and regulations are made that affect our lives and the lives of generations to come. We should always and forever take an active stand in selecting those who help make bills become laws and regulations.

White women have had the right to vote since 1920, and Black women since the Voting Rights Act of 1965, yet the political offices that women hold are still minimal at best. As for political power, women have as much political power that they are willing to pull together, vote for, and use. Each woman, 18 years and older, has one vote just as a man does. It's high time that women began to use it. Stop leaving the judicial system in the hands of men only. It's time that women make their numbers work to and for their advantage.

Think of the future. Look at the past and look at the big picture. Think about the people who have been in power in the past and ask yourselves, "What did they ever do for women, all women?" After you answer that question, look at who's now in public office, and ask yourselves what can you do to help make your communities, cities, states, and country better under new leadership?

Get out, get involved, and contribute your support for common goals. Don't leave your fate in the hands of men making decisions that affect all women. There are more female heads of households in this country than ever before, and certainly they need the same rights and equality as men working in the same jobs. Women can't buy bread and milk any cheaper than men. Yet, there are more women feeding and caring for children, many the product of broken homes, abandonment, and one-night stands. The courts are controlled by men. The child-support system is controlled by men. Many times, women are victimized twice in this society, yet, women don't seem to be mad enough to pull their numbers together and make a change in government.

The future of women is still in the hands of men. I urge women to get involved and pool their votes to take a stand. Look at the present conditions concerning women and ask yourself if you can afford to remain silent the rest of your life. Think of your children and fight to have a say in what kind of future they will have. It's time for all women, regardless of color, language, nationality, or creed, to pull together and fight for causes that affect all women and all children. Have a say in the world you leave for your children.

$\tilde{\tilde{}}$
19

*It's none of my business, but...
food handlers in restaurants
should handle food as though
they were cooking for and serving
the public, not their families.*

When I was a little girl, my grandmother
used to bake biscuits and loaves of bread. Each
time she made bread, she gave me a small portion
of dough to knead so that I could bake my own little
biscuits. However, no matter how hard I tried, my
little biscuits were always tan or brown from dirty

hands before I could bake them. I was very puzzled by the dirty looking tan tinge that was on my dough, so I asked my grandmother why were my biscuits brown before I baked them and hers were not. She looked at me patiently and said, "Darling, you have to scrub your little hands thoroughly, trim your nails real close, and wash your hands again if you're going to bake some good bread."

I said, "But Grandma, you made a mistake, you said wash your hands twice." "No mistake baby," she said. "Unless you're going to eat those little biscuits all by yourself, you can never wash your hands too much."

I think the word cleanliness should be brought to the attention of restaurant owners and managers. I believe people forget that there is a difference between preparing food for the public and preparing food at home for themselves or their families.

I recently ordered breakfast at a drive-in at a well-known restaurant in Houston, Texas. I ordered two biscuits, plain. I stopped at the first window and paid the clerk for the biscuits; then I drove to the second window to pick up the food. As I reached my hand out of the car window to grab the bag from the restaurant worker, I noticed his hands. I suddenly felt sick to my stomach. The restaurant worker had a black substance under his finger nails, and one of his fingers looked black and bruised as though it had been closed in a door or injured otherwise. Also, on each of his fingernails were white-yellowish, dried, crusty cuticles. I was appalled at the sight of his hands. As I drove home, I asked myself, "In what capacity did he work in the restaurant? Did he make the biscuits? Did he wrap the biscuits? Was he a cook at all? Was he a janitor?"

By the time I got home, I was too sick to eat. I dropped the bag into the trash and looked up the number for that restaurant's location. I asked to speak with the manager and after what seemed about ten minutes, a woman came to the phone and introduced herself as the manager. I explained how appalled and physically sick I was after looking at the hands of one of her employees in the restaurant. I explained to her, from a customer's point of view, how important it is to feel that the food you are about to eat has been prepared under clean, sanitary conditions. I told the manager that every manager of a restaurant should have a "hands" inspection of his employees on a daily basis. People with sores and germy-looking hands should not be allowed to work with food for the public.

After I talked with the manager of that

particular restaurant, I decided to visit several fast food restaurants where a customer can see the food preparation area. I witnessed a manager of another popular fast-food restaurant working the cash register, then running to the food preparation area to help the cook speed up orders without washing his hands or wearing gloves. After working on hamburgers at the fixing board, he wiped his hands on a towel and began working at the cash register again. People should never work with money and serve food at the same time without washing their hands.

At two local pizza restaurants, I noticed food handlers making pizzas with rings on and without gloves. Every time someone works with dough with rings on their fingers, they leave imprints of the jewelry in the dough. It is both unsightly and unsanitary. The chances of a food handler sanitizing, sterilizing, or disinfecting rings on his or her hands are slim. No food handler fixing pizzas wore gloves.

I bring this to the forefront not to criticize, but, out of consideration for the people who order food in public places and who are entitled to have that food prepared and served under clean, sanitary conditions. I wish the health department in every city would require food handlers to wear gloves, not just any gloves, but clean gloves that are changed after each use. I need to emphasize the former statement, because some food handlers put on a pair of gloves and do everything in that one pair of gloves without ever changing them.

I watched a young girl at a bakery counter in a grocery store in Houston, Texas, ring up customers with gloves on, put the pastry items in the bakery case with the same gloves on, and then pick up a dish towel and glass cleaner and proceed to clean the glass on the bakery case. She, then, stopped cleaning the glass and asked me if I was ready to order, all with the same gloves on. I must mention that gloves should not replace hand washing. Fingernails should be cut short so that food does not become embedded under them, and hair nets should be worn.

A food server should resist every effort to put his or her hands directly on the food that they are preparing or serving. Eating out of the pot, licking fingers, eating off customers' plates, and picking up someone's food with bare hands should be restricted to your family and home if you must do one of the above. Kitchen utensils as well as gloves represent a million dollar industry. I say to food handlers, "Please use them."

Most states require hairdressers to take a physical and have a TB test done annually to renew their beautician's license, yet, the people

who prepare food don't have to undergo any medical examinations. There's something wrong with that picture.

~~
20

It's none of my business, but...
one is never too old to learn and
never too old to go to school.

So many times I hear people say they wish
they had done something years ago, but they either
talked themselves out of it at the time or allowed
someone else to talk them out of it. Nevertheless,
time passed, nothing was accomplished, and the
person was still sad and lamenting about what
could have been.

I, too, was one of those people who used to

wish I had gone to college. There, I stood in my hair salon day after day cutting and curling the hair of working men and women who came to the salon to get their hair done and, in many cases, unburden themselves about the woes of their important jobs and fabulous careers. No matter how much some complained or bragged, I still found myself feeling that I had missed out on something crucial and special by not having finished college myself. I wanted a clean, flexible; yet, important career.

I listened to people intensely, sometimes wondering what my life would have been like if I had finished college and chosen a path with unlimited opportunities for me to make money and be happy about my job. I told my husband that I was beginning to daydream about being in a pristine job, pushing papers for a living rather than having my hands in suds, dandruff, hair, and water all day. I guess I began to wonder too much, because in 1989, I closed my salon, enrolled my daughter in kindergarten, and headed for college as a freshman. I prayed that God would give me the strength to walk out of the hair salon business and never look back. It was truly the work of God that I was able to walk away from a paying job (making cash money every day) and put myself in a student environment without any money and without the possibility of any real money for at least three years. I was uncertain as to how hard it would be to commit to something that took that long to achieve without any guarantees. The only thing that I was certain about was that I wanted to be a novelist no matter how long it took. I wanted to go to lunch like and with Barbara Taylor Bradford. She had been a guest speaker for a luncheon at a River Oaks' Social Club, and the *Houston Chronicle* newspaper had done a colorful journalistic piece on her. I cut the article out of the paper and put it in a scrapbook, because her image and public life mirrored what I dreamed of for myself.

I remember the first time I told someone I wanted to be a novelist. I could hear the snicker that the person was trying to hold back. This was before I attended college. I was still a hairdresser. There I stood, working in her head, rolling her hair, talking about wanting to become a novelist. She just couldn't imagine it and she didn't know what to say to me. I could barely imagine it in my mind and vision, but the desire burned so deeply in my heart that I couldn't ignore it. I didn't know where to start. I just knew I had to put a foot out front and take a step in the direction that I wished to go.

I enrolled in Houston Community College and took a script-writing class and a creative-writing class. I had never written anything but articles on hair and the hair industry at that point. I had to drop the script-writing class due to a family crisis, but I stayed in the creative-writing class long enough to write a never-ending story. I listened to a lot of other writers who read their work, but I did not know how to chart a story with action the way they did. Determination led me to another writing teacher who taught from her home. The first night in class I read from this huge 240-page novel I had written. The teacher stopped me on page five. She couldn't take anymore. She looked directly at me and said, "I'm going to let you have the truth cause I can see the desire to write in your eyes." At that point, she explained to me the mechanics of how to create and chart a story to bring the reader along so that a reader could see the characters, identify with the characters, see what they felt, and live vicariously through these characters. From her class, I was able to write and complete my first short story. I left her class after four months in route to college to pursue a degree in English.

While attending Texas Southern University as a freshman, I also returned to Houston Community College to take the script-writing class over. I just had to finish it. I stuck with it and wrote my first movie script that I still hope to sell one day. I was very proud of myself for going back and retaking the course I had dropped. There is a significant amount of satisfaction that comes from sticking with something to the end.

With determination, I completed a Bachelor's of Arts degree from Texas Southern University exactly three years from the semester I started. On May 13, 1995, I acquired a master's degree in telecommunications from the same university. I can proudly say from desire came hope, and my hope was in God. I believed that if I had faith, plus determination, persistence and endurance, God would give me the desires of my heart.

I can proudly testify that you are never too old to go after your dreams. I actually enrolled in college in my thirties. I still want to be invited to lunch as a novelist with Barbara Taylor Bradford, Alice Walker, and Toni Morrison. I won't stop until I am.

~~21~~

It's none of my business, but... sometimes big brother should be watching.

One of the most disappointing realities of college life is that over thirty-five percent of the freshmen population is lost each year. Early on, the warning signs of absenteeism begin to blare around the freshmen who just won't make it if they are left to their own hands. Instead of attending classes, they spend time trying to make college a social playground for themselves. The first time away from home for some, they spend their time partying and having fun in search of themselves, forgetting and losing sight of why they are really there. It's time for colleges and universities to make class attendance for the freshmen compulsory.

The university should put a firm hand on the freshmen at the beginning of the semester before they fail. The cost of books and necessary supplies should be added to the cost of tuition to ensure the freshmen will have the necessary tools needed to participate in the classes. Too often students spend weeks into the semester without books. Without books or class attendance, freshmen have no idea about what is going on in their courses. Test scores are subsequently lower and turning in homework is non-existent.

The university needs to act as a surrogate parent and protect the freshmen from themselves and their new-found freedom. The university should make the student aware that absenteeism is not going to be tolerated. The registrar's office should give the instructors pre-addressed, pre-stamped, post cards to send to the freshman's parents or next-of-kin listed on the freshman's financial information to inform them when the freshman has missed two class days. The instructor should indicate that more than three absences from a class may jeopardize the freshman's overall grade in a class. All parties involved should know early on if the freshman is wasting time and money.

The university should limit a freshman's option to withdraw from a class and receive a W as a grade. If the freshmen knew they could not withdraw from a course, they would have to put forth more effort during that course in order to pass it. It seems that all during the sixteen-week-period, that last day to drop a course and receive a "W" stands out and reminds freshmen that when they have failed, they still have that lasting "W" option.

Considering that thousands of freshmen across the country will be going back home after each semester or to work full-time for the first time, or just hang out until they find a new avenue to venture, perhaps the universities need to take away many of the choices which burden freshmen. No matter what the freshmen say about their rights, if the end results of the freshmen's decisions are flunking, withdrawing from courses, and just using college as a social incubator, then a new approach with a more stern overseer is necessary. Why not take away important decisions that will ultimately affect the freshman's academic outlook and subsequently his future. It may leave a lot of freshmen protesting at first, but as they continue school and become graduating seniors in three to four years instead of five or more years, they'll discover that commitment and full participation yield success.

~~
22

It's none of my business, but... athletes should be treated like ordinary people when it comes to drug-testing.

There are millions of people using illegal drugs each day. The majority of these people are never tested for drugs, and some of them make life and death decisions that affect other people's lives. Laws are not the same for everybody in this country. The rich and affluent are still very much the law and decision makers. Casual drug use among the rich has been accepted, almost legally. I have never seen or heard of the police hand-cuffing a house full of rich/famous people for having bowls of cocaine sitting on the coffee table at a party. Until everyone is tested for drugs and fired if found using, I don't think athletes should be tested and fired either. A professional athlete should be given the same number of chances as all other employees to stop using drugs, if his job performance has been affected, before he is put out of professional sports.

As long as the athlete can perform the job he is paid to do, he should be allowed to do it. Athletes require stamina and must be in great physical shape to be able to perform at a professional level. Long-term drug use takes a physical toll on the human body that prevents the body from reaching excellence. When an athlete can no longer perform at the standard at which he was hired, he should be fired for that reason, not the drug test results.

The sports leagues should stop the drug testing of their employees until every company and organization in America test their members and employees for drugs. The number of people that the athletes can hurt in the process of doing their job performance is less than most people in state-funded jobs can hurt. School bus drivers, teachers of young children, doctors, nurses, IRS auditors, judges, jurors, and policemen are just a few of the many groups who should be tested for drugs and monitored on a regular basis because their job performance seriously affects other people.

The reasons for drug use and abuse varies from person to person, and there is no infallible prescription for stopping drug use. Firing an athlete because of drug use, or approaching him about drugs even though his job performance is satisfactory is not fair unless the rest of American workers are tested. Expecting them to be role-models for our children is too much for any group of people to ask of another. We should never ask nor expect any more of the athletes than we expect of ourselves. We created and condoned the salaries they earn. We bought into the hype generated by the press. We put athletes on pedestals when their feet should have been firmly on the ground; but now, it's time to humanize them, take away the illusions and fantasies, and allow those athletes to be real, like ordinary people should be.

~~ 23

It's none of my business, but... the tongue is mightier than the sword, and people should be careful what they say to others because they just may get insulted back.

There are no perfect people in this world. God is a "just" God. He gave all of us something we can be proud of. We were not all supposed to look alike nor act alike; therefore, no one, especially famous people, should try to insult or ridicule someone else's looks. Famous people are constantly in the public eye and should certainly understand whomever they talk about and whatever they say will have a stronger, more astounding impact on an audience. Famous people who verbally ridicule other people do a great disservice. They should use their fame to promote constructive causes. Besides, there are some things famous people have criticized others about that would take an act of God to change. Things like the shape of someone's head or their adult height are out of the person's control. Therefore, to continue to criticize at this point would be considered malicious and painful.

Arsenio Hall should not have ridiculed people for laughs, because some Americans did not laugh. If he had thought about the people he ridiculed for a few moments, I believe he would have agreed that personal attacks on people <u>are no laughing matter.</u>

In order to host the show, he needed to develop a nightly monologue. Apparently, he thought, to be funny, he had to put down others. He launched a fat-joke campaign against Roseanne Barr and Oprah Winfrey. He threw in jokes about Robin Givens without mentioning that Robin's husband was his friend. Robin Givens and Oprah

Winfrey chose to publicly ignore Arsenio regardless of the pain. However, Roseanne got tired of his verbal cuts and stabs and retaliated with her own definition of what that kind of humor was. Roseanne said, "Fat jokes are as painful as racism, and maybe Arsenio Hall can understand that and say, 'enough is enough.'" She went on an HBO special and referred to Arsenio Hall as an "Eddie Murphy Kiss-ass." She has also referred to him as "triangle face." Surely name-calling can result from famous people making unkind comments about other famous people.

Joan Rivers is another famous person who used her television platform as a medium for hurling insults and put-downs to her, supposedly, good friends. The major recipient of her abuse was Elizabeth Taylor. Joan never talked about how many husbands Liz had had because that fact would have given credence to Liz in a different light. Joan's hate campaign only highlighted something Liz couldn't change instantaneously, her weight. Joan said in her monologue, "Liz Taylor is so fat, that when she had her ears pierced, gravy ran out." Joan's follow-up joke to that was that while Liz was ordering at Mac Donald's Restaurant, the numbers on the sign that reads, 'billions served' kept changing. The audience roared with laughter, but somewhere, many people were not laughing. Years later, Elizabeth Taylor said on a Barbara Walter's show that she died inside every time she was the butt of somebody's fat joke on television. She said that if she were fat, that was her own personal pain. No one had a right to say anything about it. It just wasn't funny to her.

David Letterman is another famous person who should stop hurting people verbally. He is using his good fortune as an opportunity to stick it to people who are not there to defend themselves at the time. Sometimes you can verbally slip up when you are cultivating a nasty, spiteful, destructive personality and say things in front of the person you're criticizing. When David Letterman's show was on NBC, he insulted Florence Henderson on his show one night, after asking her about her childhood. Florence told him that she came from a poor family, but they always had love. She went on to talk about the level of her family's poverty. David Letterman said that he always thought he was poor, but they were rich compared to Florence's family. David laughed, and the audience moaned in surprise. Florence Henderson looked startled before she calmly told David Letterman that if his family were so rich, why didn't his parents fix his teeth?

Those little cuts and stabs actually hurt people. People should always say in their minds whatever they are about to say <u>before</u> they say it aloud to anyone else. Just ask yourself if you would appreciate it if what you're thinking is said to you.

Some people would say that verbal ridicule and comedy acts about famous people are just a part of being famous. Others would say it is a stolen license for slander, spite, and pain. I believe it is unproductive because everyone has a mountain to climb in his or her life at one time or another and tries to overcome the struggle within self and triumph as a complete person. However, what that mountain is varies from person to person. No two people necessarily have the same problem, but as sure as there is a God, there is a mountain to climb for everyone. The incline could be a little less steep if we gave each other a boost, verbally, emotionally, physically, or otherwise rather than laughing at or ridiculing each other for having the mountain to climb in the first place. The fact that we all have mountains in our lives is true, and some can identify and name some mountains easier than others. That, too, could be a plus, not something to be joked about, because if the person's problem is readily identifiable like fat, baldness, big-nosed, little eared, crooked teeth, and on and on, half of his battle is won. No one should speak on those areas of someone else's appearance, because in hurling verbal insults, the tongue is mightier than the sword. Even those folks who don't have any visible problems, please be assured that they do have problems, probably buried. The question becomes, how deep?

Everyone should keep in mind that if he has five or ten minutes to spare on criticizing or insulting someone, he should take those few minutes and look at and look inside himself and start with his suggestions on self first. Always spend the extra time on correcting self. There would be less time to drop-kick and insult other people.

~~ 24

It's none of my business, but... parents should know that they cannot pay people to love their babies.

To say one cannot pay anyone to love one's baby may sound harsh and negative, but the fact of the matter is there is a real possibility that no one in the world will love a child like a child's parents. Every child has a unique cry that is familiar to his parents. That special unique cry can tug at a parent's heart in a way that makes a parent respond automatically to the needs of his or her child. That same cry may not have any effect at all on the baby-sitter or care giver of the same child.

Over the years, I gave up searching for good quality child care for my first child, and never attempted to look for child care ten years later with my next child. During my initial search, I encountered too many instances where sitters and child care institutions were just not right. In visiting child care institutions, I noticed babies lying in playpens and cribs all day long with their hair rubbed off the backs of their heads and toys piled upon them to amuse them rather than the comfort and benefits of human contact. I could not entertain the idea of leaving a child under the age of two in a child care institution for that very reason. It seemed that none of the workers in the institutions that I visited wanted to hold babies. Every one of the workers described a crying baby as "being spoiled." I was horrified by such a thought. To me, a baby wanting to be held is a normal function. It was terrible to me for grown women to refuse to hold a baby because they actually believed holding a baby was going to spoil him even further. Why would a person agree to work at a child-care facility and not want to nurture a child? I knew then that I would budget to the bare bones before leaving my infant in any child care institution.

Another complaint was children getting lost in a circle of too many children per child-care worker. One child-care-giver for at least fifteen children in most instances is down-right horrible. Surely, there are going to be children who are not hugged or held during the day. No child should be without loving arms all day.

One of the main things most parents worry about in child care is abuse: whether a child is physically or sexually abused. However, there are other kinds of abuses such as too many kids put together without adequate supervision causing many of the kids to get pushed around and fought by other children. You also have the mental abuse of a child not being nurtured and causing a child not to feel loved in an environment that he or she spends most of his day. A child having to fight over a toy all day everyday can't be good for a child's emotional state of being.

Over the years, I have encountered numerous women in the position of having to locate good child care for their children. I was told a countless number of times that children were neglected at the babysitter and in child-care institutions by not being fed a meal more than once a day and not having their diapers changed but once a day. Standard child-care institutions offer one lunch around 11:00 a.m. and a snack around 2:00 p.m.

That's all. There are parents who drop their young children off at a child-care institution at six or seven in the morning and don't pick them up until 5:00 P.M. or later. Those children are no doubt very hungry by the time they leave with a parent. The sad part comes when the parents don't immediately have cooked food available for the kids. Some kids don't eat until dinner time. The administrators of child-care institutions should be ashamed to ration food to small children, but countless numbers of them do.

Women who leave their children at the homes of care-givers have additional things to worry about that parents who leave their children in institutions don't have to think about. One serious thing is that a lot of home care-givers take their clients' children with them while they run errands to grocery stores, doctors' offices, laundry mats, and where ever they need to pay a bill or make a stop. Many times, these children are left in the automobiles while the home care-givers run in and out of the stores. Not only is that dangerous in the traffic and crime-ridden shopping areas, but the temperature of the weather can be a factor to the children. Children have died from heat exertion in the summer, and children have been seriously affected by the cold in the winter when they are being driven around town while their parents are at work thinking their kids are safe at the home care-givers.

I personally recalled finding a truck-load of crying, screaming kids on the parking lot of a local grocery store. I walked over to the vehicle because I could not ignore the screams of the children. There was what seemed to be a 10-year-old boy covered in sweat sitting in the truck holding a crying, newborn infant, while a toddler of about two-years old sat on the floor of the truck, and three other children, all under the age of four, sat on the seat of the truck crying. The temperature was at least 98 degrees here in Texas. I felt that whoever was driving that truck was supposed to be baby-sitting because the children inside the truck were of different races and many seemed to be the same age. I asked the 10-year-old boy where his parents were, and he told me his mother was in the grocery store. I questioned him, and he gave me her name. I went directly to the manager of the grocery store and told him what I had encountered on the parking lot. He paged the woman, who at the time was nearing the register. She smiled and said, "I'm the woman you paged." At that point, I looked directly into her eyes, and said, "Lady, you should be ashamed of yourself to leave those babies in that hot truck while you shop in this air conditioned store."

She still tried to smile as she said, "I left my

son out there with them. They're all right."

"I said, Lady, those children are screaming, crying, and drenched in sweat, and that infant should never be exposed to 98-degree weather." Before I could say anything else, she looked at me and said that same stupid statement that I am so tired of hearing, "That baby is just spoiled. She's all right."

I told the manager that he should call the police. At that point the lady quickly handed the cashier her money and said she was leaving the store. I told her that I wish I knew the names of those babies' parents because I would personally call them and tell them the kind of day their children were having with this home-care-giver.

Child-care institutions are businesses, and child-care givers are workers in a business. Caring for children is their job, and we know the world is filled with people who go to work every day and not only do not like their jobs, they don't do their jobs well. They find ways to cut corners and do as little as possible. Unfortunately, too much of that goes on in child-care institutions, whether it is a daycare in someone's house or in a shopping center or a commercial building. There are people working in daycares who offer no love to the very children they are paid to care for.

~~
25

It's none of my business, but... everyone should realize that on any given day their lives could depend on the competence and care of strangers.

     Michael Jackson with all of his millions was suddenly on his back, unconscious, when someone on the stage dialed 9-1-1. The E.M.S. (Emergency Medical Services) of New York City came to save his life. At that moment, not Michael's bodyguards, not his publicists, not his agents, not his sponsors, not his adoring fans, not Liz Taylor, nor any of the other legends he surrounds himself with were there to save him. Strangers, everyday people, probably working for less than $50,000 a year came to save his superstar life.

On any given day, neither of the people in their E.M.S. uniforms would have been able to get close enough to Michael Jackson to get his autograph for the "little people" are always kept at bay, but when Michael's life depended on the "little people," they were suddenly able to actually touch the "King of Pop." I have to wonder if Michael's bodyguards frisked the E.M.S. attendants before they were allowed to touch the "King of Pop?"

For those of you who may think I'm picking on Michael Jackson, I say, "Nothing could be further from the truth." I admire Michael's talent as I do many entertainers, but I am a little sick of one group of people behaving as though they're more important than God. The truth is everyone fitting under the heading of "celebrities," including athletes should remember they were born into this world like everyone else and they, too, will die like everyone else. Celebrities behave as though there is some isolated world just for entertainers and famous people when they die. I don't think so.

I'm waiting to hear one day that celebrities will erect their own "Celebrity E.M.S. Agency" so they can be resuscitated by their own kind, but of course, you have to be famous or have millions of dollars to be one of their E.M.S. attendants. Maybe each celebrity will take a turn volunteering to save the life of his own kind. But then, their egos will probably get in the way or contract negotiations will take place over the phone lines while the sick celebrity's life lay at bay.

The rich already don't eat with the common folk of the world. They buy their own restaurants, dedicating the first floor to the poor and common folk, so their $10 bills for a burger can pay for the second floor of the restaurant that is exclusively for the rich owner and his own kind.

Michael requested the hospital to rearrange the I.C.U. (Intensive Care Unit) by moving every "sick" body off "his" unit. The hospital administrator was undoubtedly as "sick" as Michael Jackson because the last media report said patients were scheduled to be moved. What was Michael afraid of...germs? Didn't he know that he brought germs into the hospital as a patient, himself. Was Michael afraid the other sick I.C.U. patients were going to crawl out of bed, IV's and tubes intact and ask him or his famous friends for an autograph? Or did Michael think the sick patients wanted to take his picture? It seems that knocking at death's door didn't bring down that snob barrier that automatically kicks in when some people make their first million or with some celebrities, even less.

I implore those people who could be considered "adoring fans" of anyone to please leave those "snob" celebrities alone — completely— literally, figuratively, and financially. Never let people think they have to hire a body guard to keep you away from them. People who don't want to be bothered with you, please reciprocate the feeling by ignoring them totally.

It's none of my business, but... I just want to say that in the end...rich and poor, famous and unknown, people all exit this world the same...through death.

~~

26

It's none of my business, but... I believe people are humanly unlimited.

To keep saying or writing over and over that this is a white man's world and, no matter how hard people try, he is still going to win is the worst form of negativism possible; and to keep repeating it, perpetuates doom for all people. Thus, it becomes despair personified. People must stop this kind of thinking.

A glimmer of hope is desperately needed, be it an illusion, a dream, or just a self-made justifiable concept to enable us to believe we can win or over come. We must stop saying we can't do this or that because we are Black and "the man" is not going to let us do it. Truly, the odds are in favor of the offense. If we continue to strike the door—pushing, insisting, and persisting—it is then up to the oppressor to defend the territory in question. Our job as a people is not to help the oppressor guard the door by continuing to keep ourselves oppressed with negativism and disbelief. It is we who should perpetuate hope for each other by saying, "yes we can," while we offer each other a hand. We have a God-given right to every door that has ever opened in this world.

If it were ever done anywhere in the world by anybody, it can be done by any one of us. We have an obligation for our future to look at the accomplishments of the world and the achievements of humans everywhere and to know that we, too, as humans, have the same opportunities within ourselves to accomplish whatever we undertake. All we need in common with the next achiever is the fact that we are all humans. All people must stop putting themselves into boxes and containers.

If someone is living your dream, they don't have to be the same race as you to know that you can live the dream too. Mentors can come in any color or gender. You don't even have to know your mentor personally. You can study him from afar.

Never doubt your HUMAN connections or capabilities. Rely on them first. After we have accomplished our quest, it is great to seek out fellow peers pursuing the same endeavors regardless of their color or creed. We can learn from a model even though it does not resemble us in any form other than human. The color of the achiever is not what validates us as hopefuls or contenders. The humanness is the equalizer.

Don't mentally entertain the idea that someone won't allow you "in." If you believe that, you're doing the work for an oppressor. You're hindering yourself. If you do that the oppressor doesn't have to shut you out. You're shutting yourself out. You should continue to push the door, because you're trying to get in. Make the oppressor spend his life trying to keep you out. Don't do it for him. Your job is to keep trying to get in. Let's see who will get tired first. We have grown up hearing stories about relentless Black people and their God-given capabilities to endure suffering longer than anyone else; so, let's see if we can take that myth and use it as the advantage it was meant to be.

Too long Black people have lived with "The Invisible Wall" that other races claimed they couldn't see and whites claimed they didn't put up.

Yet, Black people were told by some whites in the beginning what lines they could and could not cross. Then, the true disaster occurred when Black people began to teach their children what lines they could and could not cross. Black people began passing the word around about Blacks staying in their places within the realms of their white-given territories. Blacks taught other Blacks about the "invisible wall" until, suddenly, the "man" did not have to keep reminding us. Blacks are guarding the "wall" for him.

Black people began to move within that "allowed frame" and many stopped attempting to cross the line. I ask you to ask yourselves when was the last time you tried to cross over the "invisible wall?" When was the last time you applied for anything that people, black or white, told you that you weren't ever going to get because you are Black, a woman, too short, too tall, too aggressive, or too fat. When did you last test the wall? Was the wall there in reality or was it there only in your mind? And what's the difference? Have you ever crossed the wall and felt surprised or good that you did get over? Did you feel liberated? Were you glad you tried?

Black people must deprogram their destinies. Wipe out negativism and restraints from the past. The constitution says, "All men are created equal." It didn't say all men are treated equal. The treatment is up to you. You have a responsibility to determine how people treat you. To say all men are created equal says to me that God has done his part. It's up to me to acknowledge EQUALITY in my soul and mind and personify it fully by believing I have the same opportunity as any fellow human.

First, you must know, without a doubt that you are equal. The rest of your life is up to you. It becomes CHOICE, your choice, from that point to eternity. We have to refuse to be restricted by the pains of denial inflicted upon our ancestors. They chose, some of them individually, to feel helpless in accepting the inhumane treatment inflicted upon them by their white slave masters. We have a choice to accept or reject the treatment of man, regardless of a man's color.

We don't have to take abuse from anyone. The only person who has a right to judge your worth is God and, if you communicate your heart to Him, He can lead you to everlasting life. We were created equal by God and should never wear any shackles, invisible or otherwise, because of color, sex, or creed.

Since this is the era of "just say no," we can just say no to an unequal, unfulfilling life and say yes to making our lives exactly what we want without reference to color, sex, or creed, but with reference only to the hearts of equal human beings.